I0815594

Ceratopsians

Horned-Face Dinosaurs

by Grace Hansen

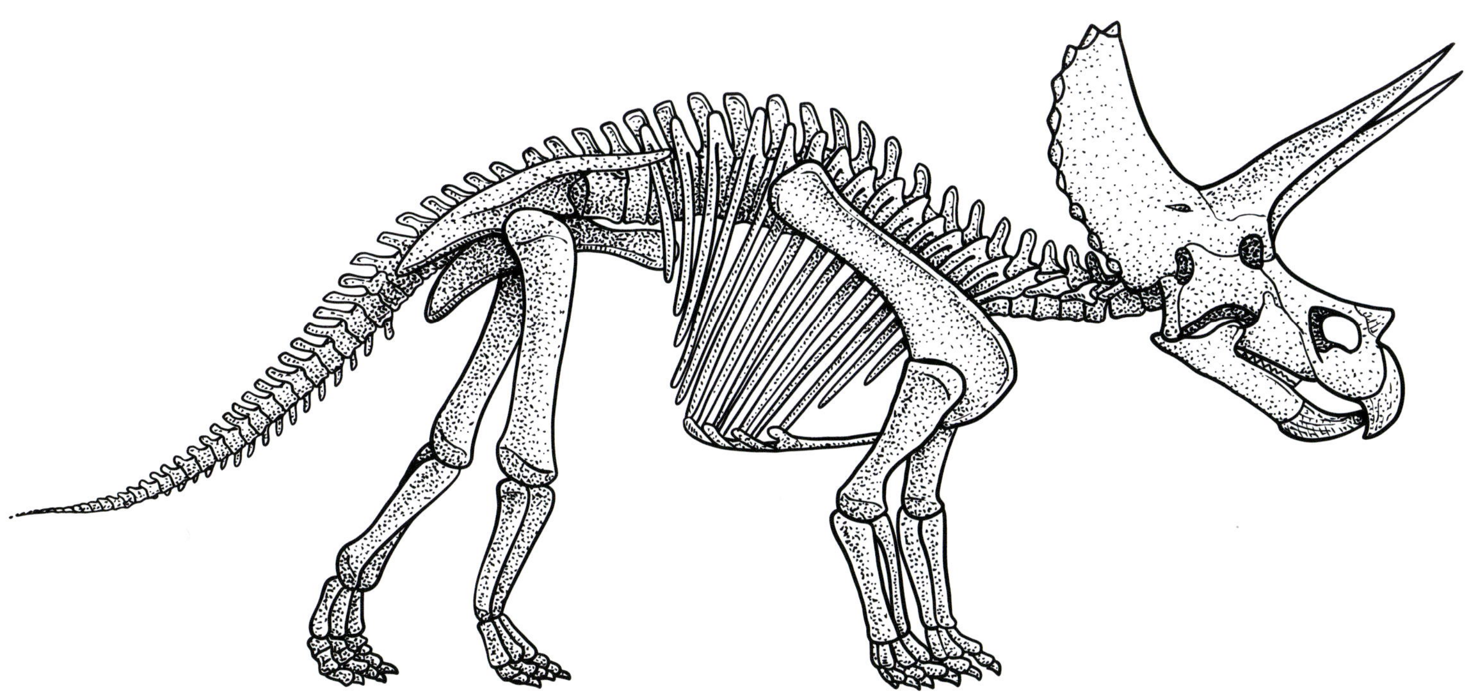

Abdo Kids Jumbo is an Imprint of Abdo Kids
abdobooks.com

abdobooks.com

Published by Abdo Kids, a division of ABDO, P.O. Box 398166, Minneapolis, Minnesota 55439.

Printed in the United States of America, North Mankato, Minnesota.

052025

092025

Photo Credits: Adobe Stock, Alamy, Getty Images, Science Source, Shutterstock

Production Contributors: Teddy Borth, Jennie Forsberg, Grace Hansen
Design Contributors: Candice Keimig, Pakou Moua

Library of Congress Control Number: 2024947607

Publisher's Cataloging-in-Publication Data

Names: Hansen, Grace, author.

Title: Ceratopsians: horned-face dinosaurs / by Grace Hansen

Other Title: horned-face dinosaurs

Description: Minneapolis, Minnesota : Abdo Kids, 2026 | Series: Dinosaur groups | Includes online resources and index.

Identifiers: ISBN 9798384905158 (lib. bdg.) | ISBN 9798384905851 (ebook) | ISBN 9798384906209 (read-to-me ebook)

Subjects: LCSH: Dinosaurs--Juvenile literature. | Prehistoric animals--Juvenile literature. | Animals, Fossil--Juvenile literature. | Paleontology--Juvenile literature.

Classification: DDC 567.90--dc23

Table of Contents

The Horned-Face Dinosaurs

Ceratopsians were a group of dinosaurs. They mainly lived during the Cretaceous period. They were found throughout North America, Asia, and Europe.

Jurassic
201 million
years ago

Cretaceous
145 million
years ago

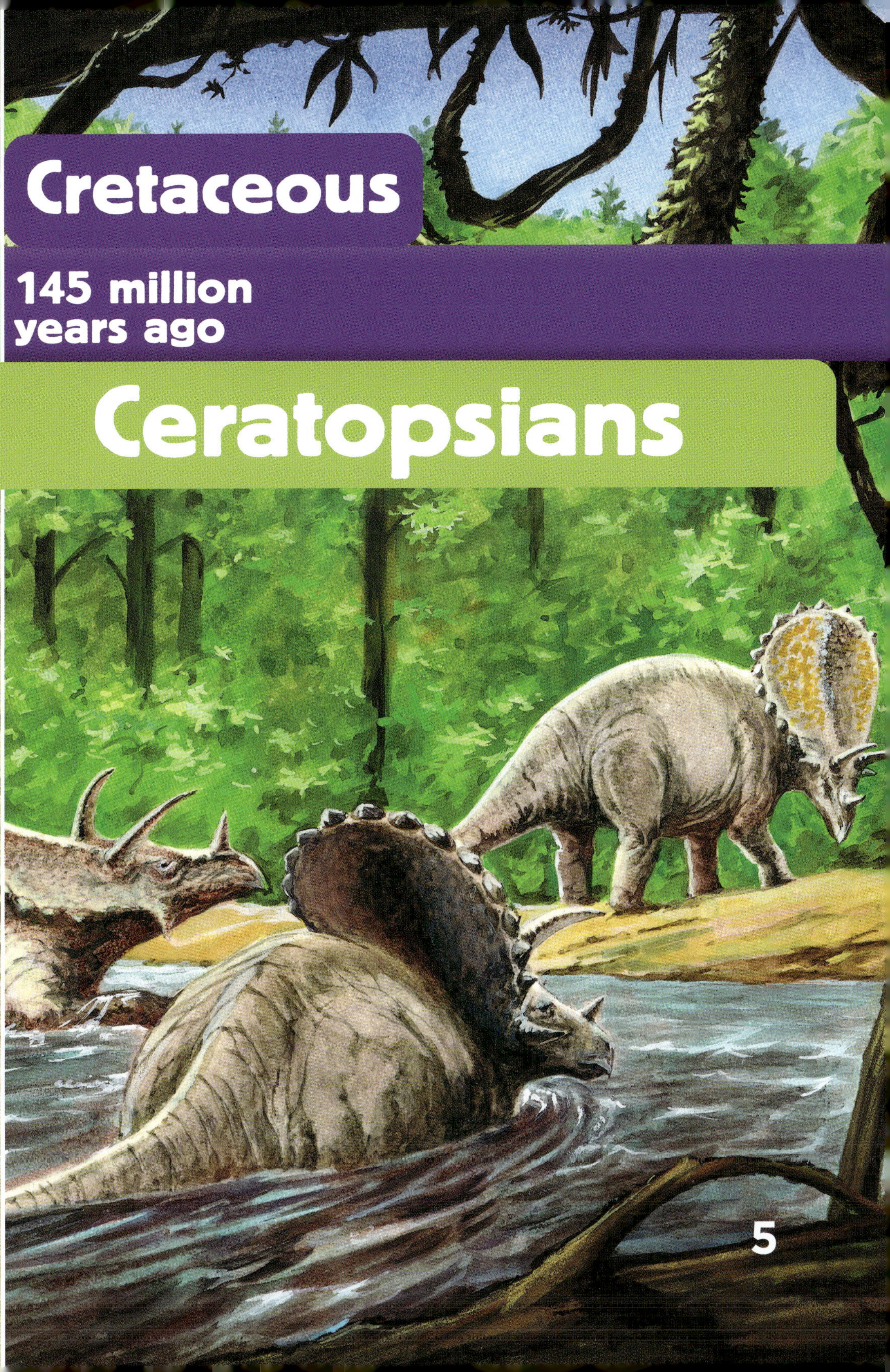

Ceratopsians

The earliest ceratopsians were small. Some walked on two legs. They had a small **frill** and no horns.

Later ceratopsians were much larger. They had to walk on four legs. They had a large **frill** and often had horns.

Pentaceratops
Centrosaurus
Not a Dinosaur
Yinlong
Sinoceratops
Triceratops

Ceratopsians are known for their **frill** and **unique** skull. The frill may have protected them against attacks. It may have also kept them cool or attracted **mates**.

Ceratopsians were **herbivores**. Their beak helped them pluck leaves from trees and bushes. Their teeth were good for **grinding** up tough plants.

Einiosaurus

Einiosaurus was a medium-sized ceratopsian. It is known for its downward-curving **nasal** horn. Two spikes **extended** from its **frill**.

Late Cretaceous
Fossils found in
North America
As long as an
orca
20 ft (6 m) long
As heavy as a
small sedan
3,000 lbs
(1,360 kg)
Einiosaurus

Styracosaurus

Styracosaurus means "spiked lizard." The dinosaur lived up to its name. Its **nasal** horn was straight and about 2 feet (.6 m) long. It had horns **extending** from its cheeks and even more from its **frill**!

Styracosaurus
Late Cretaceous
Fossils found in
North America
As long as
2 ping-pong tables
18 ft
(5.5 m) long
As heavy as
2 female hippos
6,000 lbs
(2,720 kg)

Torosaurus

Torosaurus had the largest **frill** of any ceratopsian. Its skull was larger than any other land animal. It had two horns above its eyes and a small **nasal** horn.

Torosaurus
Late Cretaceous
Fossils found in
North America
As long as a
small airplane
25 ft
(7.6 m) long
As heavy as a
school bus
SCHOOL BUS
16,000 lbs
(7,260 kg)

Triceratops

The largest and most famous ceratopsian is the *Triceratops*. It had three horns and a large **frill**. It lived in forested areas and open **plains** where it could find plenty of food.

Late Cretaceous
Fossils found in
North America
As deep as an
NFL end zone
30 ft (9 m) long
As heavy as
2 Asian Elephants
20,000 lbs
(9,070 kg)
Triceratops

Common Ceratopsian Features

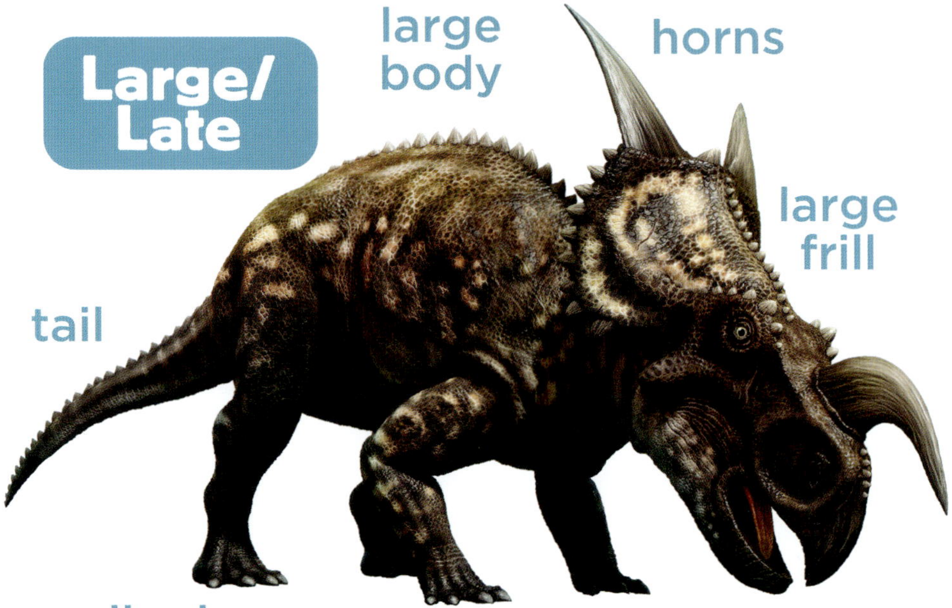
Large/ Late
large body
horns
large frill
tail
walked on all fours
beak-like mouth

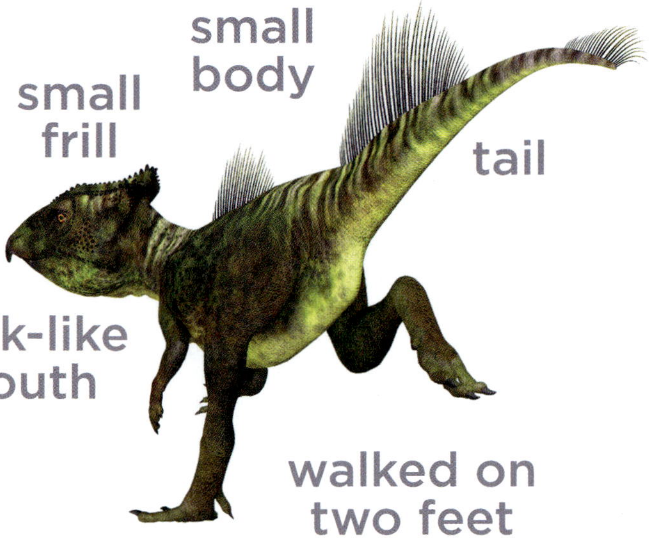
Small/Early
small body
small frill
tail
beak-like mouth
walked on two feet

Small/ Late
tail
small body
small frill
beak-like mouth
walked on all fours
ran on two feet
large head

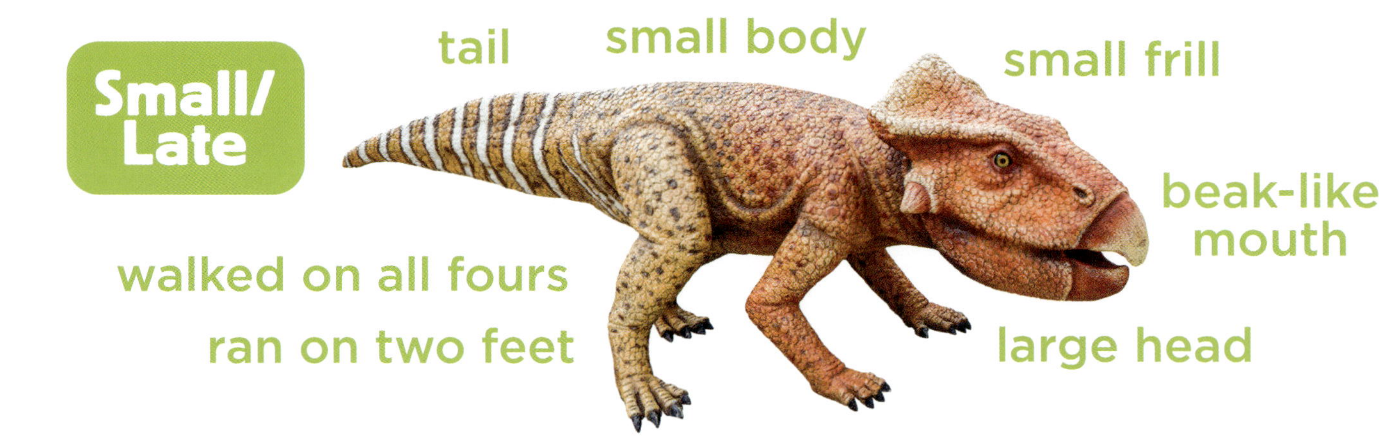

Glossary

extend – to stretch out.

frill – the large, bony plate on the back of a dinosaur's head.

grind – to crush into very small pieces.

herbivore – an animal that only feeds on plants.

mate – one of a pair of animals that have young together.

nasal – of the nose.

plain – a large, flat area of land with few or no trees.

unique – being the only one of its type.

Index

Visit **abdokids.com** to access crafts, games, videos, and more!

Use Abdo Kids code

DCK5158

or scan this QR code!